Learning Short-take®

NEGOTIATING FOR SUCCESS

The process and tools for win/win

CATHERINE MATTISKE

TPC - The Performance Company Pty Ltd
Level 20, Darling Park
Tower 2, 201 Sussex Street,
Sydney NSW 2000
Australia

ACN 077 455 273
email: tpc@tpc.net.au
Website: www.catherinemattiske.com

© TPC – The Performance Company Pty Limited
First edition published in 2006
Second edition published in 2011
Third edition published in 2022

All rights reserved. Apart from any fair dealing for the purposes of study, research or review, as permitted under Australian copyright law, no part of this publication may be reproduced by any means without the written permission of the copyright owner. Every effort has been made to obtain permission relating to information reproduced in this publication.

The information in this publication is based on the current state of commercial and industry practice, applicable legislation, general law and the general circumstances as at the date of publication. No person shall rely on any of the contents of this publication and the publisher and the author expressly exclude all liability for direct and indirect loss suffered by any person resulting in any way from the use of or reliance on this publication or any part of it. Any options and advice are offered solely in pursuance of the author's and the publisher's intention to provide information, and have not been specifically sought.

For eBook version: By payment of the required fees, you have been granted the non-exclusive, non-transferable right to access and read the text of this e-book on screen. No part of this text may be reproduced, transmitted, downloaded, decompiled, reverse engineered, or stored in or introduced into any information storage retrieval system, in any form or by any means, whether the electronic or mechanical, now known or hereinafter invented, without the express permission of the author.

A catalogue record for this book is available from the National Library of Australia

National Library of Australia
Cataloguing-in-Publication data

Mattiske, Catherine
Negotiating for Success: The Process and Tools for Win/Win

ISBN 978-1-921547-22-5

1. Occupational training 2. Learning I. Title

370.113
_____

Distributed by TPC - The Performance Company - www.catherinemattiske.com
For further information contact TPC - The Performance Company, Sydney Australia on +61 (02) 9555 1953.

HELLO.

Welcome to the Learning Short-take® process!

This Learning Short-take® is a bite sized learning package that aims to improve your skills and provide you with an opportunity for personal and professional development to achieve success in your role.

This Learning Short-take® combines self study with workplace activities in a unique learning system to keep you motivated and energized. So let's get started!

Step 1:
What's inside?

- Learning Short-take®. This section contains all of the learning content and will guide you through the learning process.
- Learning Activities. You will be prompted to complete these as you read through.
- Learning Journal. This is a summary of your key learnings. Update it when prompted.
- Skill Development Action Plan. Learning is about taking action. This is your action plan where you'll plan how you will implement your learning.

Step 2:
Complete the Learning Short-take®

- Learning Short-takes® are best completed in a quiet environment that is free of distractions.
- Schedule time in your calendar to complete the Learning Short-take® and prioritize this time as an investment in your own professional development.
- Depending on the title, most participants complete the Learning Short-take® from 90 minutes to 2.5 hours.

Step 3:
Meet with your Manager/Coach

- Schedule a 30 minute meeting with your Manager or Coach.
- At this meeting share your completed Activities, Learning Journal and Skill Development Action Plan.
- Most importantly, discuss and agree on how you will implement your learning in your role.

GET VIP ACCESS
TO YOUR MATERIALS

This Learning Short-take® includes an interactive activity book, associated tools and job aids, plus a bonus eBook.

1 Visit
https://www.catherinemattiske.com/books

2 Select your book

3 Click: **VIP ACCESS**

4 Enter the code: **NFS2022277**

WELCOME

Negotiating for Success
The Process and Tools for Win/Win

Negotiating for Success combines self-study with realistic workplace activities to develop skills in successful negotiating. This Learning Short-take® is particularly relevant to those who are new to negotiating or who would benefit from strengthening negotiation skills. You will learn how to effectively prepare for a negotiation using your own real life business opportunity and how to incorporate key steps and elements into the negotiation process. You will identify how to achieve a win/win outcome in a negotiation and will be able to differentiate positional bargaining from principled negotiation.

Negotiation is an ever-present feature of both our personal and professional lives, and in the business world effective negotiators are in high demand. Bringing a complex negotiation to a successful conclusion can be one of the most individually exhilarating and valuable aspects of business today.

Negotiating for Success includes the **Negotiation Planner**, provided as a free downloadable tool.

Now let's get started!

1	Learning Short-take® > Start here
2	Learning Journal 65
3	Skill Development Action Plan 71
4	Quick Reference 77
5	Next Steps 99

"In business, you don't get what you deserve, you get what you negotiate."

CHESTER L. KARRASS

"

The freedom of the city is not negotiable. We cannot negotiate with those who say, 'What's mine is mine and what's yours is negotiable.'

JOHN FITZGERALD KENNEDY

"

Section 1
LEARNING SHORT-TAKE®

WHAT'S IN THIS LEARNING SHORT-TAKE®

"The fellow who says he'll meet you halfway usually thinks he's standing on the dividing line."

ORLANDO A. BATTISTA

Table of Contents

How to Complete Your Learning Short-take®	5
Activity Checklist	6
Learning Objectives	7
Let's Get Started	8
Part 1 - Negotiation Defined	9
Win/Win Model	15
Principled Negotiation Requirements	22
Part 2 - Preparing for Negotiation	25
Part 3 - The Negotiation Process	31
Element 1 - Interests	33
Element 2 - Inventing Options for Mutual Gain	35
Element 3 - Standards	40
Element 4 - People	45
Element 5 - BATNA	53
Element 6 - Close	60
Part 4 - Summary	61

HOW TO COMPLETE YOUR LEARNING SHORT-TAKE®

1. Follow this Learning Short-take® by **actively reading each section and highlighting key points** as you go.

2. When directed, stop and complete activities.

3. When directed or at any time, **stop and update your Learning Journal (located with your activities).**

4. Meet with your Manager/Coach to review your progress and establish an action plan. Ensure you have completed all activities, updated your Learning Journal and created your Skill Development Action Plan.

5. Subject to your coach's final review and assessment, you will either sign off the Learning Short-take® as complete, or undertake further skill development as appropriate.

"Let us never negotiate out of fear. But let us never fear to negotiate."

JOHN FITZGERALD KENNEDY
(AMERICAN 35TH US PRESIDENT)

ACTIVITY CHECKLIST

"We're eyeball to eyeball and the other fellow just blinked."

DEAN RUSK

During this Learning Short-take® you will be prompted to complete the following activities:

- Activity 1 - Initial Skills Self-Assessment   13
- Activity 2 - Negotiation Situations   18
- Activity 3 - Preparation Reflection   28
- Activity 4 - The Sisters and the Orange   36
- Activity 5 - Standards - The Case for Objective Criteria   41
- Activity 6 - Standards - Developing Objective Criteria   42
- Activity 7 - Writing Questions for Negotiations   50
- Activity 8 - BATNA - Yes, But…   58
- Activity 9 - Final Review   63
- Learning Journal   65
- Skill Development Action Plan   69

LEARNING OBJECTIVES

- Define negotiation - what it is and what it isn't.
- Explain the win/win model of negotiation.
- Differentiate between positional bargaining and principled negotiation.
- List the steps in preparing for a negotiation.
- Identify and explain the steps in the negotiation process.
- Define BATNA.
- Apply the Negotiation Planner Tool to a real-life negotiation.
- Create a Skill Development Action Plan.

"If you can't go around it, over it, or through it, you had better negotiate with it."

ASHLEIGH BRILLIANT
(ENGLISH AUTHOR AND CARTOONIST, B.1933)

LET'S GET STARTED

"People tend to resist that which is forced upon them.

People tend to support that which they help create."

VINCE PFAFF

Most people find themselves involved in negotiation as an essential part of work life. For some this may become one of the most significant and time consuming aspects of their role.

This Learning Short-take® aims to identify and examine different negotiation techniques, and to start to identify negotiation strategies that are most likely to prove successful.

Whether you are negotiating with an external customer, internal customer, your manager or peers, sound negotiating skills are an essential part of business communication.

The Learning Short-take® will assist a wide audience including managers, sales people, customer service staff, trainers, marketing, finance, internal consultants or any other business role.

This Learning Short-take® will help those with responsibility for purchasing, personnel, contractual work, or any other role where the ability to reach a negotiated agreement or settlement is important.

NEGOTIATION DEFINED

PART 1

NEGOTIATION DEFINED

*"There are two fools in every market.
One asks too little, one asks too much."*

RUSSIAN PROVERB

Introducing Negotiation

Negotiation is the means by which people deal with their differences. Whether those differences involve the sale and purchase of a home, an employment contract dispute, a dispute with a client, or making trade-offs on internal resources, resolutions are typically sought via the process of negotiation.

Most business people negotiate something on a daily basis.

To negotiate is to seek mutual agreement through an exchange of dialogue.

Negotiation is an ever-present feature of both our personal and work lives, and in the business world effective negotiators are in high demand.

Bringing a difficult negotiation to a successful conclusion can be one of the most individually exhilarating and organizationally valuable aspects of business today.

Sales vs. Negotiation

The process of selling and negotiating are two very different things.

Selling involves interacting with prospective customers and offering them products or services that fulfill their needs.

Negotiation is the process whereby two or more parties consent to bargaining, in order to arrive at a mutually acceptable solution regarding the rate of exchange of specific items or services. In addition to arriving at a mutually acceptable solution, relationship building between the parties is a significant objective of the negotiation process.

Traditionally, the ability to negotiate has been considered a skill for salespeople only. In reality however, it is a skill that we all use on a regular basis - at work, home, with colleagues, family, friends etc. From major issues to minor details - everyone negotiates.

"Negotiation in the classic diplomatic sense assumes parties are more anxious to agree than to disagree."

DEAN ACHESON

What negotiation isn't

Successful business people have learned that negotiation is about trade-offs, and achieving a "win-win." And sometimes the "win-win" may be different from what you originally thought you wanted.

The end game in negotiation isn't getting your way, it's constructing a "deal" that satisfies the needs and wants of everyone.

Combining Sales & Negotiation

If you are a sales person who negotiates the two definitions combine.

Negotiation plays an important role in effecting a successful sales process. It helps in achieving the sales objectives without making the other party concede too much.

In other words, effective negotiation helps in developing a 'win-win' situation for the buyer and the seller.

Complete Activity # 1
Initial Skills Self-Assessment

ACTIVITY 1 - INITIAL SKILLS SELF-ASSESSMENT

Understanding the key elements of negotiation is critical to improving job and sales success This assessment covers the key skills for successful negotiating.

Rate yourself on each of the techniques.
7   is competent and confident, little need for improvement
4   is average, needs improvement
1   is uncomfortable, major need for improvement

- Note specific areas of improvement related to each that you would like to develop. Be sure to include your **reasons** for your rating in each skill, as this reasoning will be a key part of the initial goal setting session with your coach.
- Start thinking about a personal development plan and identify two or three things you could do to improve your skills in this area and write them in the space provided.

I...	Rating	Reasoning
Differentiate between selling and negotiating depending on the situation	1 2 3 4 5 6 7	
Understand and use win/win	1 2 3 4 5 6 7	
Use principled negotiation rather than positional bargaining	1 2 3 4 5 6 7	
Prepare for every negotiation in written form, consulting others where necessary	1 2 3 4 5 6 7	
Use negotiation tools and forms on a regular basis	1 2 3 4 5 6 7	
Focus on the other party's interests to avoid positional bargaining	1 2 3 4 5 6 7	

ACTIVITY 1: CONTINUED

I...	Rating	Reasoning
Seek options and numerous possibilities when structuring the agreement	1 2 3 4 5 6 7	
Use many different creativity techniques when negotiating, including brainstorming, six thinking hats and others	1 2 3 4 5 6 7	
Research objective criteria prior to a negotiation to present if required	1 2 3 4 5 6 7	
Keep negotiation issues and relationships in balance during a negotiation	1 2 3 4 5 6 7	
Develop a BATNA prior to a negotiation	1 2 3 4 5 6 7	
Use various closing techniques to gain commitment	1 2 3 4 5 6 7	

Personal development plan ideas:

1

2

Now update your Learning Journal (page 65)

WIN/WIN MODEL

In his book Seven Habits of Highly Effective People, Stephen Covey discusses the concept of win-win. Habit 4 - Think Win/Win discusses six paradigms of Human Interaction. We've created the model (right) showing how the concepts measure up against two drivers - courage & consideration.

Win/Win
- Agreements or solutions are mutually beneficial.
- A belief in the Third Alternative - A *better* way.

Win/Lose
- Use of position, power, credentials, possessions or personality to get one's way.
- The win/lose mentality is dysfunctional to interdependence.

Lose/Win
- Lose/Win people are quick to please or appease.
- Capitulation - giving in or giving up.

Many executives, managers and parents oscillate between Win/Lose and Lose/Win.

"No one should negotiate their dreams. Dreams must be free to fly high.

No government, no legislature, has a right to limit your dreams.

You should never agree to surrender your dreams."

JESSE JACKSON
(AMERICAN CIVIL-RIGHTS LEADER, BAPTIST MINISTER AND POLITICIAN, B.1941)

Lose/Lose
- Result of encounters between two Win/Lose individuals.
- Also the philosophy of highly dependent people.

Win
- Win at all costs. Other people don't matter.
- The most common approach in everyday negotiation.

Which Option is Best?
- Most situations are part of an interdependent reality.
- Win/Win solutions are synergistic.

Win/Win can lead to No Deal
- If we can't find a solution that would benefit both parties, we agree to disagree.
- Most realistic at the beginning of a relationship or enterprise.

5 Dimensions of Win/Win

1. Character. The foundation of Win/Win
- Integrity. The value we place on ourselves.
- Maturity. The balance between courage and consideration.
- Abundant Mentality. There is plenty out there for everybody.

2. Relationships. Courtesy, respect and appreciation for the other person and their point of view.

3. Agreements. Cover a wide scope of interdependent action.
- Desired results
- Guidelines
- Resources
- Accountability
- Consequences

4. Supportive Systems. Reward systems must reflect the values of the mission statement.

5. Processes. The route to Win/Win:
- See the problem from another point of view.
- Identify the key issues and concerns involved.
- Determine what results would constitute a fully acceptable solution.
- Identify possible new options to achieve those results.

Complete Activity # 2
Negotiation Situations

ACTIVITY 2: NEGOTIATION SITUATIONS

Using the model as a guide, list examples in the table below of negotiations that have resulted in:

```
High |  Lose / Win          |  Win / Win or No Deal
     |                      |  Win / Win
Consideration
     |                      |
     |  Lose / Lose         |  Win / Lose
Low  |                      |  Win!
     Low      Courage           High
```

You/Them	Definition	Situation	What was the short-term outcome?	What was the long-term outcome?
1. Lose/Lose	Both Parties Lost			

ACTIVITY 2: CONTINUED

You/Them	Definition	Situation	What was the short-term outcome?	What was the long-term outcome?
2. Lose/Win	You lost, the other party won			
3. Win/Lose	You won, the other party lost			
4. Win	You won, however either had no regard for, or didn't know whether the other party won or lost			
5. Win/Win	Both parties won			
6. Win/Win or No Deal	Where you walked away because both parties couldn't win, or you stated clearly that this was your intent and negotiated a win/win outcome			

Now update your Learning Journal (page 65)

Positional Bargaining vs. Principled Negotiation

Positional Bargaining Defined. Positional bargaining is essentially **adversarial.** The negotiators see the process as "win-lose," in which any gains by the opponent are losses by the home team. There are definite winners and losers in this type of negotiation.

'Hard' Positional Bargaining

Positional bargaining can be illustrated by the purchase of a new car or real estate. We might see some of the following traditional and conventional tactics used on both sides during selling a car or real estate - in fact they could relate to many sales, or negotiations!

- The salesperson has a sticker price to begin with.
- The customer has a desired purchase price.
- Each wants to get as close as they can to their own figure.
- The salesperson's commission is based on the profit margin achieved, directly from the customer's pocket.
- The customer wants the lowest possible profit margin, directly from the salesperson's commission.
- Each gains at the other's expense.
- It is adversarial.

This is an example of "hard" positional negotiation. The negotiators are demanding and unyielding.

'Soft' Positional Bargaining

Positional bargaining can also be "soft." A "soft" bargainer is quite willing to make concessions to "keep the ball rolling."

- The two negotiators start at different positions in a bargaining range and compromise toward the middle.
- In "soft" bargaining, agreements are reached quickly.
- However, "soft" bargainers run a great risk if they happen to encounter a "hard" bargainer.
- Furthermore, "hard" and "soft" bargaining may result in 'splitting the pie' or 'splitting the difference' in order to get what they want. This is the ultimate position of weakness because this outcome is rarely based on facts, and rarely meets the needs of either party resulting in either a 'that will do' outcome, or lose/lose.

In Summary - Positional Bargaining

In all positional bargaining, each side stakes out its position, and simultaneously

- attacks the other position and
- defends its own.

The goal of every effective negotiator is to get the opponent onto their side of the bargaining table, so viewpoints will be similar.

PRINCIPLED NEGOTIATION REQUIREMENTS

"Start out with an ideal and end up with a deal."

KARL ALBRECHT

Principled negotiation has four conditions which are essential if the negotiation is to have a successful outcome.

1. Mutual trust.
2. A positive relationship.
3. Shared interests (goals or objectives).
4. Satisfactory zone of possible agreement.

1 - Mutual Trust

Mutual trust comes from experience, either within the negotiation process or from previous contact. If it does not already exist, it must be built. A negotiator can be trusted when experience shows that person:

- is dependable and will do what he/she promises to do, and
- does not create surprises.

Surprises can take many forms: a sudden demand "out of the blue," a sudden opponent's threat, or an unexpected shift in position, which negatively impacts credibility. One of the objectives of a negotiator is to establish his/her credibility in the eyes of the other negotiator.

As a negotiator, your goal is to have more influence on the other side than they have on you. Your goals and objectives must be seen to gain merit while the goals and objectives of the other side lose merit. This means your presentation of "facts" and other evidence must be convincing. You must also create some doubt in the mind of the other negotiator about the validity of his/her position.

In essence, you will be influencing that person to take your position. A positive relationship with the other negotiator is essential if you are to have this kind of influence. Even though this may sound difficult, experienced negotiators emphasize that it is both possible and necessary.

> *"The greatest misunderstanding about the negotiation process is that it is adversarial in nature. In actuality, it is not designed for those with a trial and debate mentality. It is a problem solving process in which each party may look across the table and regard its counterparts as [potential] advocates."*
>
> COLOSI

2 - Positive Relationship leading to condition 3 - Shared Interests

A positive relationship makes possible the development of common ground. In principled negotiation the common ground can include similar goals and objectives. Instead of negotiating against each other, the negotiators negotiate "against" the problem. The negotiators now have shared interests.

4 - Zone of Possible Agreement (ZOPA)

Finally, a Zone of Possible Agreement (ZOPA) must exist. This may appear to apply more to positional than to principled negotiating because a ZOPA is the least favorable agreement you would accept, and the most favorable one you believe the other negotiator would accept. ZOPA can shift negotiations in a positive direction, however be careful not to become too locked into a ZOPA process, as it may restrict negotiating options and possibilities.

The Walk Away Position - BATNA

A negotiator must also have a Best Alternative to a Negotiated Agreement (BATNA). As part of the preparing for negotiations, you should decide at what point it is best to cease negotiating and to be satisfied. Although the BATNA may change slightly as negotiations proceed, a negotiator will use the BATNA as a checkpoint throughout the negotiation process. With a BATNA a negotiator rarely feels cornered or under pressure to yield to pressure from the other side.

PREPARING FOR NEGOTIATION

PART 2

PREPARING FOR NEGOTIATION

How to Prepare for a Negotiation

To prepare for a negotiation, gather information about your interests, resources and alternatives, and about your counterpart's. Determine your Best Alternative to a Negotiated Agreement (BATNA, at what point are you prepared to stop negotiating, and what you would get if you walked away from the negotiation), set your goals of the negotiation, and then attempt to assess your counterpart's goals and BATNA. Research different sources and query outsiders for objective facts.

For example, say you are getting ready to negotiate with prospective employees. Before you sit down with any applicants, be sure you've asked some questions of HR, other managers, and key stakeholders, such as: "How much do you pay for this role? What kind of benefits do they get? What is the retention rate in this position? How can we make the position more attractive to applicants?"

Getting Started with Preparation

Before you begin, you might prepare a list of potential negotiating points.

Begin with critical and obvious issues, and then try to imagine spheres into which the agreement might extend.

Establish the value you place on each issue, and the value your opponent is likely to place, looking both for areas where your interests coincide and for potential trade-offs.

Be careful not to lock on to a fixed idea of what your counterpart's needs and interests are. You need to remain receptive to new information that becomes available in the course of the discussion.

For example, if you are negotiating a marketing agreement with a possible supplier, and your counterpart is authorized to sign off on the deal, be sure that you also have that ability. But, if your counterpart must run any proposal by colleagues before signing, then be certain that you also reserve that option.

Complete Activity # 3
Preparation Reflection

ACTIVITY 3: PREPARATION REFLECTION

Consider a recent negotiation experience and answer the following questions.

1. Were you worried about the outcome of the negotiation?

   _____

2. How much time did you spend in preparing for the negotiation?

   _____

3. What did you do to prepare for the negotiation?

   _____
   _____

4. Did you assess the needs/motives of the customer?

   _____

5. Did you consider bottom lines?

6. What was the outcome of the negotiation?

   _____
   _____

7. As you look back on the situation, were you adequately prepared?

   _____
   _____

ACTIVITY 3: CONTINUED

8. What would you do differently if you were just beginning your preparations now?

_____
_____
_____
_____
_____

9. If you implemented these preparations, what possible difference would this have made to the outcome?

_____
_____
_____
_____
_____
_____

Now update your Learning Journal (page 65)

NEGOTIATION PLANNER

Within this Learning Short-take® is the Negotiation Planner. This tool will assist you in negotiations. Download it now. You will use the Negotiation Planner to prepare for an up-coming real life negotiation.

 Download the Negotiation Planner from https://www.catherinematttiske.com/books

Activity using the Negotiation Planner

Think of an upcoming 'real life' negotiation and complete **only** the following sections of the Negotiation Planner…

- Section 1 - General Information

You will create the remaining parts of the Negotiation Planner later.

Any business arrangement that is not profitable to the other person will in the end prove unprofitable for you. The bargain that yields mutual satisfaction is the only one that is apt to be repeated.

B. C. FORBES

THE NEGOTIATION PROCESS

PART 3

THE NEGOTIATION PROCESS

1. Interests
2. Options
3. Standards
4. People
5. BATNA
6. Closure

> *Any business arrangement that is not profitable to the other person will in the end prove unprofitable for you. The bargain that yields mutual satisfaction is the only one that is apt to be repeated.*
>
> B. C. FORBES

ELEMENT 1 - INTERESTS

Positions

Positions are generally the concrete action or item you want. Focusing on position rather than interests can lead to a "line in the sand" approach in which both parties end up with only sand. Hence the term, as previously discussed in this Learning Short-take®: Positional Bargaining.

- Things you say you want
- Demands
- Terms and conditions

About Positions

- Never take positions for granted
- Always look behind positions for the underlying interests

"If you are planning on doing business with someone again, don't be too tough in the negotiations. If you're going to skin a cat, don't keep it as a house cat."

MARVIN S. LEVIN

Interests

Interests are intangible motivations that lead you to take a particular position - your needs, desires, concerns, fears, and aspirations. Interests are often revealed when one explores the true underlying motives of each party. The more interests are known, the more options can be considered in negotiation. Effective negotiation considers shared interests as well as those in conflict.

- Underlying motivations
- Needs and concerns
- Fears and aspirations

About Interests

- Understand your interests before continuing a negotiation

Uncovering Interests

- Look behind positions for underlying interests
- Put your self in the other person's shoes
- Ask "why?"
- Ask "why not?"
- "What could be wrong with...?

 Use the downloaded Negotiation Planner from https://www.catherinematttiske.com/books

Activity using the Negotiation Planner

Think of an upcoming 'real life' negotiation and complete **only** the following sections of the Negotiation Planner...

- Section 2 - Goals & Objectives
- Section 3 - Positions & Interests

You will create the remaining parts of the Negotiation Planner later.

ELEMENT 2 - INVENTING OPTIONS FOR MUTUAL GAIN

Overcoming Obstacles

Options are all of the many possibilities for structuring the agreement. The most creative options are those that satisfy the interests of both parties. They solve a problem or enhance an opportunity.

Sometimes this opportunity is one that neither party was aware of until the brainstorming of possible approaches to address mutual interests began.

Options include the original ideas as well as all new possibilities considered for addressing the problem.

Four major obstacles that inhibit the inventing of options

1. Pre-judgment

2. Searching for the single answer

3. The assumption of fixed parameters

4. Thinking that "solving **their** problem is **their** problem"

Complete Activity # 4
The Sisters and the Orange

ACTIVITY 4: THE SISTERS AND THE ORANGE

This is the story of two sisters who quarrelled over an orange. They had one orange and they both wanted it. They argued at length and finally agreed to divide the orange in half.

The first sister took her half, ate the fruit and threw away the peel. The other sister took her half, threw away the fruit and used the peel to bake a cake.

The point is that both sisters wanted different parts of the orange. Had they identified these needs at the outset, the argument would have been short lived and they would have both ended up with what they wanted.

Too many negotiators end up with half an orange for each side instead of the whole fruit for one and the whole peel for the other.

All too often negotiators "leave money on the table".
Write your responses in your Learning Journal.

1. Why do you think this happens?
2. What should have the two sisters done at the beginning of the negotiation?
3. What might have been a question that they could have asked?
4. Reflect on a negotiation when you have walked away with a less than optimum outcome.
    a. What was the negotiation?
    b. Who was it with?
    c. What happened?
    d. How did you feel?
    e. What did you learn from the negotiation?

Now update your Learning Journal (page 65)

Increasing Creativity in Negotiations

When working with a group, the negotiation often needs structure to invent creative options. There are many different creativity techniques - brainstorming, mind mapping, 6 Thinking Hats, and others.[1]

Here are some simple guidelines to help facilitate a creative process:

- **Focus the group on the objective of the negotiation** - if they don't have an objective this is a good place to start being creative.
- **Respect the group** - no one likes to be told they have been doing it wrong, so show respect for past and current methods of idea generation. Help the group find the desire to be creative by asking questions about their future and the future of their markets, industry and customers.
- **Take your time, don't push too hard** - encourage the group to take ownership of the whole process.
- **Focus on the future** - don't dwell on current problems which are well known and serve to keep people fixed on habitual ways of problem solving.

We all have some level of creativity within us. As with other activities, you can teach yourself to be more creative. Sometimes creative thinking requires us to look at things from new perspectives. It's essential not to allow the negotiating process to become stalled.

Using formal creativity techniques allows the development of alternatives and options that are a vital part of gaining an agreed outcome when negotiating.

---

[1] Learning Short-take®: 'Creative Business Thinking' will assist you in developing your skills in methods for creativity for use in negotiations and many other business situations.

"The majority sees the obstacles; the few see the objectives; history records the successes of the latter, while oblivion is the reward of the former."

ALFRED A. MONTAPERT

Idea Growers

Idea Growers are those individuals and managers who elicit contributions by presenting problems as opportunities for input. These are the managers that everyone wants to work with. They grow their employees by encouraging input and providing feedback on projects and assignments.

Phrases that an idea grower would typically use to spark creativity and innovation are:

- What have we missed?
- What would happen if…
- What else would be affected by this change?
- What questions are there?
- Why do we do it this way?
- How could we improve…?
- and Thank You.

Idea growers stimulate creativity and conversation by true interest and compassion for their employees and team members. They use open ended questions and comments to spark more dialogue with a group of people.

How to Destroy Creativity

The goals of a negotiation can comfortably coexist with the creative process. The ability to develop creative options relies on three things: expertise, the ability to think flexibly and imaginatively, and motivation. Ensure that your next negotiation doesn't stall due to a lack of willingness to explore all options to achieve an agreed outcome.

Idea Killers

Have you ever worked for someone who is adept at finding problems but has no ideas for solutions? They expect you to come up with ideas for them to approve. You end up going back to them innumerable times, only to have them sigh in the end, apparently dissatisfied with anything you've come up with. This is normally driven by the approaching deadline which demands a decision be made.

Some common phrases or actions used by an Idea Killer are:
- That's not in the budget.
- NEXT!!
- That's not the way we do it.
- We've tried that before and it didn't work.
- It won't work.
- That's too complex for these people to understand.
- and worst of all, complete silence.

 Use the downloaded Negotiation Planner from https://www.catherinematttiske.com/books

Activity using the Negotiation Planner

Think of an upcoming 'real life' negotiation and complete **only** the following sections of the Negotiation Planner...

- Section 4 - Options

You will create the remaining parts of the Negotiation Planner later.

ELEMENT 3 - STANDARDS

Negotiation Standards - Using Objective Criteria

Negotiating parties often get stuck over whose version of the facts is true, or whose proposal is most reasonable. This is known as **Positional Bargaining** and focuses purely on what each party is willing and unwilling to accept. No amount of negotiation will produce a win/win outcome where one party pits their will against the other, and either one is forced to back down.

It's exhausting and rarely results in an outcome. You should avoid Positional Bargaining, always.

The solution is to negotiate on some basis independent of the will of either side, that is, on the basis of objective criteria.

This is known as **Principled Negotiation** and focuses on the merits of the problem, not the pressure of the parties. If you can develop a set of impartial criteria for measuring acceptability, the negotiation has a greater chance of win/win success.

Complete Activity # 5
Standards - The Case for Objective Criteria

Complete Activity # 6
Standards - Developing Objective Criteria

ACTIVITY 5
STANDARDS - THE CASE FOR OBJECTIVE CRITERIA

You have recently suffered serious accident damage to your car. In negotiating your insurance claim, your insurance assessor refers to a formula in the company's procedure manual, resulting in a figure that is unacceptably low. You on the other hand, refer to the actual cost to repair your vehicle, evidenced by several quotes from licensed local repairers. The assessor does not accept your position.

What standards have been used in this negotiation?	What is wrong with these standards?	What standards might be more acceptable in this case?

Now update your Learning Journal (page 65)

ACTIVITY 6
STANDARDS - DEVELOPING OBJECTIVE CRITERIA

Read the list of Standards in Column 1 below. These are some of the accepted standards in business today and can be used for many negotiations. It is useful to pre-research these Standards so that at your next negotiation you can use them with little or no preparation.

For each Standard record how you might apply these Standards to negotiations in your current role. Also record what other information you might need to ensure that the Standards are objective for both parties in your negotiation.

Standards accepted in business today	How you might apply these Standards in your negotiations?	What other information might you need to ensure that these Standards are objective?
Market value (perceived worth in the market)		
Precedent (tradition)		
Professional standards (accepted by the industry)		
Product Efficiency standards (product performance/quality ratings etc)		
Product Cost		

ACTIVITY 6: CONTINUED

Standards accepted in business today	How you might apply these Standards in your negotiations?	What other information might you need to ensure that these Standards are objective?
Competitor Standards		
Moral Standards (socially accepted)		
Environmental Standards		
Technological Standards		
Reciprocity (mutual give-and-take)		
Other (add your own)		
Other (add your own)		

Now update your Learning Journal (page 65)

 Use the downloaded Negotiation Planner from https://www.catherinematttiske.com/books

Activity using the Negotiation Planner

Think of an upcoming 'real life' negotiation and complete **only** the following sections of the Negotiation Planner…

- Section 5 - Standards

You will create the remaining parts of the Negotiation Planner later.

Now update your Learning Journal (page 65)

ELEMENT 4 - PEOPLE

Balance of Issues & Relationships

While it is important to focus on the issue of the negotiation, it is also important to address the relationship needs of the parties in the negotiation.

- Important that both the issue (the task at hand) and the relationship (the desire to do business again) are in balance. If not, one may feel emotionally cheated or that they did a poor job as a negotiator.
- Usually, if people do not feel good about how they performed, they will not feel committed to the deal.
- In this instance they may look for a way out.
- If the balance is right, there will be an emotional commitment to the deal and its implementation.

If the balance is right, there will be an emotional commitment to the deal and its implementation.

People Checklist for Success

- Other side - people just like you
- Be empathic and assertive
- Focus on the issue not the person
- Balance emotion with reason
- Tactfully question
- Actively listen
- Observe carefully
- Ensure mutual understanding
- Don't buy the relationship

> *"The negotiating world often contains some razzle-dazzle and hocus-pocus, so lighten up and enjoy the game."*
>
> DR PHIL

Traits of a Good Negotiator

Understand people

A good negotiator understands people. He/she has acquired a practical knowledge of human habits and behaviors, built up over a lifetime of observation and interaction. This understanding seems to be manifest in instinct and intuition. Good negotiators somehow seem to be able to anticipate or guess correctly about the other side's next action or reaction.

Exude confidence

There is something very strange about self-confidence. If you don't have it, you can't fake it. If you are not confident, no matter how good an actor you are, you won't really fool the other side for long.

On the other hand, if you do have it, it is immediately perceived by the other side.

It's almost as if having self confidence gives the negotiator an aura - the glow of assurance, the expectation of success.

Is open-minded

If you enter negotiations with a narrow, constricted view, you are probably going to be dissatisfied with the negotiating effort. In order to participate effectively in the give-and-take of negotiation, you need to be open-minded. You cannot forge a compromise if you would not be willing to accept one.

Remain calm

Negotiations can become emotional. Both sides are subject to losing control over their emotions.

It's easy to take a remark personally and respond in haste.

It's human nature to get excited, agitated, or irritated with the tone of the conversation or the selection of tactics in a negotiation.

The successful negotiator remains calm in the eye of the storm.

"Make every bargain clear and plain, that none may afterwards complain."

GREEK PROVERB

Body Language Signals

While word choice is critically important. Perhaps even more essential is how you say them. Your delivery of the message makes all the difference. Most people use the phrase 'body language' to refer to all aspects of interpersonal communication beyond the choice of words.

Everything becomes important when a message is being delivered: voice tone, volume, inflection, pace, eye contact or lack of it, facial expressions, gestures, movements or lack thereof, posture, muscle tension, changes in skin coloring, clothing, hair style, eyeglasses, and so on. Whew!

Staying aware of all aspects of body language continuously is not possible. Having some awareness is very important in becoming assertive. Even though other people might not be able to list all of your body language signals during an interaction, they respond to and interpret them unconsciously as part of receiving your message. This process is automatic, constant and complex.

Don't be discouraged. You don't have to constantly monitor all aspects of body language to be assertive. You do, however, need to learn some body language signals to accompany your words that will help you be perceived as an assertive person. Perfection is not required for success.

Following are some basic body language signals that have been categorized according to how most people perceive them.

Body Language Checklist
Posture

Non-Assertive	Assertive	Aggressive
• slumped • shoulders forward • shifting often • chin down • sitting: legs entwined	• erect but relaxed • shoulders straight • few shifts, comfortable • head straight or slight tilt • sitting: legs together or crossed	• erect, tense, rigid • shoulders back • jerky shifts or planted in place • chin up or thrust forward • sitting: hands behind head or tensely leaning forward

Gesture

Non-Assertive	Assertive	Aggressive
• fluttering hands • twisting motions • shoulder shrugs • frequent head-nodding	• casual hand movements • relaxed hands • hands open, palms out • occasional head-nodding	• chopping or jabbing with hands • clenched hands or pointing, sweeping arms • sharp, quick nods

Facial Expression

Non-Assertive	Assertive	Aggressive
• lifted eyebrows, pleading look, wide-eyed, rapid blinking • nervous or guilty smile • chewing lower lip • shows anger with averted eyes, blushing, guilty look	• relaxed, thoughtful, caring or concerned look, few blinks • genuine smile • relaxed mouth • shows anger with flashing eyes, serious look, slight flush of color	• furrowed brow, tight jaw, tense look, unblinking glare • patronizing or sarcastic smile • tight lips • shows anger with disapproving scowl, very firm mouth or bared teeth, extreme flush

Voice

Non-Assertive	Assertive	Aggressive
• quiet, soft, higher in pitch • uhs, ahs, hesitations • stopping in mid-stream • nervous laughter • statements sound like questions with voice tone rising at the end	• resonant, firm, pleasant • smooth, even-flowing • comfortable delivery • laughter only with humor • voice tones stay even when making statement	• steely quiet or loud, harsh • "biting off" words • measured delivery • sarcastic laughter • statements sound like orders or pronouncements

Complete Activity # 7
Writing Questions for Negotiations

ACTIVITY 7: WRITING QUESTIONS FOR NEGOTIATIONS

Asking questions is a key skill in negotiating for success. Practice writing questions for the situations below, changing the questioning tone as directed.

Imagine you are negotiating with your manager about your workload. You want to find out how many accounts the other service people have. You believe that you have been handling many more accounts than the others, and you are earning the same salary as they are.

1. Write a direct question with a neutral tone.

2. Rewrite the question with an aggressive or threatening tone.

3. Revise the question to give it a friendly or conciliatory tone.

4. Write an open question to get the other side talking in general on the topic.

ACTIVITY 7: CONTINUED

Imagine you are negotiating to buy a used computer. You think the asking price in too high based on your estimate of the original price. You'd like to know what the original price really was and the age of the computer.

1. Write a direct question with an aggressive tone.

_____

_____

2. Write an open question with a neutral tone, to elicit this information.

_____

_____

3. Revise the question to give it a friendly or conciliatory tone.

_____

_____

4. Write an open question to get the other side talking in general on the topic.

_____

_____

Now update your Learning Journal (page 65)

  Use the downloaded Negotiation Planner from https://www.catherinemattiske.com/books

Activity using the Negotiation Planner

Think of an upcoming 'real life' negotiation and complete **only** the following sections of the Negotiation Planner…

- Section 6 - People

You will create the remaining parts of the Negotiation Planner later.

Now update your Learning Journal (page 65)

ELEMENT 5 - BATNA

Develop Your BATNA -
Best Alternative to a Negotiated Agreement

Your BATNA is not Your 'Bottom Line'

Negotiators often try to protect themselves from a bad deal by establishing in advance, the worst acceptable outcome - their 'bottom line'. Having a bottom line makes it easier to resist the pressure and temptation of the moment. For example, for a potential home buyer the bottom line is the highest price they will pay. The amount is determined in advance and prevents them from making a decision they may later regret.

Your BATNA is the standard against which any proposed agreement should be measured.

However, the protection afforded by adopting a bottom line involves high cost. It limits your ability to benefit from what you learn during the negotiation. By definition, a bottom line is a position that does not change. It is decided in advance and unmoved by what the other party has to say.

A bottom line also inhibits imagination during the negotiation process, preventing the parties from inventing a solution that is more advantageous to both. If you insist on a bottom line it is unlikely that you will explore alternate creative solutions, preventing you from agreeing to a solution that you would be wise to accept.

Know your BATNA (Walk Away Position)

Your BATNA (Best Alternative to a Negotiated Agreement) is the standard against which any proposed agreement should be measured. This is the only standard that protects you from accepting terms which are unfavorable, and from rejecting terms that you would be wise to accept. It is also flexible enough to permit the exploration of creative alternatives.

Take for example the sale of a home. When deciding on the minimum sale price for a house, the vendor typically asks the agent: "What price should I be able to get?" This in turn leads to a decision about the bottom line. However, what the vendor should really be asking themselves is: "What will I do if I cannot sell the house in a given period of time?" This leads to a variety of options such as renting it out, tearing it down and rebuilding etc. It may be that one of these options is more attractive than selling the house in the first place. The point is that it is highly unlikely that any arbitrarily selected bottom line truly reflects the vendor's real interests.

Plan your BATNA

Exploration and planning of what you will do if you do not reach agreement can greatly strengthen your position in the negotiation. Generating possible BATNA's requires four distinct activities:

1. Inventing options that you might consider if no agreement is reached.
2. Improving some of the more promising ideas and converting them into practical alternatives.
3. Tentatively selecting the option that you believe is the best.
4. Considering the other party's BATNA so that you can better estimate what to expect from the negotiation and prepare accordingly.

How to Negotiate with a Customer You Can't Afford to Lose

The Aim

- Find a creative way to satisfy both the other party in the negotiation and you in **Principled Negotiation**
- Refuse to fight but refuse to let the customer take advantage of you. Hold your ground. **Aim for Win/Win or No Deal.**

Know your walk-away position and build the number of variables offered.

- Before negotiating you must know your Best Alternative to a Negotiated Agreement (BATNA).
- The more variables you have to work with the more you have to offer, the greater your chance of success.
- Focus on variables where the customer's interests and yours have more in common.
- For undifferentiated products increase the variables by focusing on services.

When under attack, LISTEN!

- Avoid an upward spiral of heated disagreement.
- Collect as much information as possible from the customer.
- Listen carefully for the customer's underlying agenda (the iceberg principle).

Keep the customer talking.

- New information can increase the room for movement and number of variables.
- Listening without defending helps to defuse any anger.
- If you are listening you are not making concessions.

Keep track of issues requiring negotiation.

- Summarize what has already been accomplished and sketch out what still needs to be discussed.
- Brief infrequent recaps actually help maintain momentum and reassure customers that you are listening to their arguments.
- Neutralize outspoken opposition by converting objections into issues that need to be addressed.
- Wait patiently for a calm moment to summarize your progress.

Assert your needs!

- Principle of "sticky fingers" - bargaining requires a dual focus.
- If you fail to assert your needs you may too readily make unnecessary concessions.
- Aim to build common ground by emphasizing shared interests, avoiding inflammatory language and encouraging discussion of disrupted issues.

Commit to a solution only after it's certain to work for both parties.

- Suggest hypothetical solutions to avoid appearing to be digging into a position.
- Invite the customer to help shape the proposal.
- Don't agree definitively to an issue without making sure the overall deal still makes sense. Wrap up issues tentatively.

Save the hardest issues for last.

- Resolving relatively easy issues first creates momentum.
- Discussing easier issues may uncover additional variables.

Start high and concede slowly.

- High expectations produce the best negotiating results and low expectations the poorest.
- Always get something in return for concessions and know their economic value.
- Concede things that the customer values highly but has little incremental cost to you.
- Concede in small increments, get something in return and know the concession's value to both sides.

Complete Activity # 8
BATNA - Yes, But...

ACTIVITY 8: BATNA - YES, BUT...

1. What does BATNA stand for?

2. Why is it suggested that establishing a 'bottom line' is detrimental to the negotiation process?

3. Why is the party with the best BATNA also the more powerful party in the negotiation?

4. Why is it important to try to estimate the other side's BATNA?

Now update your Learning Journal (page 65)

 Use the downloaded Negotiation Planner from https://www.catherinematttiske.com/books

Activity using the Negotiation Planner

Think of an upcoming 'real life' negotiation and complete **only** the following sections of the Negotiation Planner…

- Section 7 - BATNA

You will create the remaining parts of the Negotiation Planner later.

Now update your Learning Journal (page 65)

ELEMENT 6 - CLOSE

- Think about closure before you begin
- List the issues of both sides
- Draft a framework
- Improve as you go
- Create emotional commitment
- Fill in details before you commit
- Don't commit until the end

Negotiation isn't about winning, it's about success.

 Use the downloaded Negotiation Planner from https://www.catherinematttiske.com/books

Activity using the Negotiation Planner

Think of an upcoming 'real life' negotiation and complete **only** the following sections of the Negotiation Planner…

- Section 8 - Closure

Congratulations. You have now completed the Negotiation Planner and this should help you in your upcoming negotiation.

Now update your Learning Journal (page 65)

SUMMARY

PART 4

SUMMARY

- Most people negotiate most days.
- A negotiation should result in Win/Win based on Principled Negotiation techniques.
- Preparing for all negotiations is essential.
- Using the 6-step negotiation process will keep you on track.

Complete Activity # 9
Final Review

ACTIVITY 9: FINAL REVIEW

1. What is the difference between positional bargaining and principled negotiation?

2. What is one way of testing for objective criteria?

3. What are some commonly accepted Standards in business today?

4. What are three important points that you should keep in mind when establishing objective criteria?

5. What does BATNA stand for?

6. What is the definition of BATNA?

7. List three ways to close a negotiation

Now update your Learning Journal (page 65)

To be successful, you have to be able to relate to people; they have to be satisfied with your personality to be able to do business with you and to build a relationship with mutual trust.

GEORGE ROSS

Section 2
LEARNING JOURNAL

The Learning Journal is used throughout the process to record your key learnings, hot tips and things to remember.

Update your Learning Journal at anytime. Ensure you complete your Learning Journal after you finish each activity. Then turn back to the Learning Short-take® to continue your learning.

LEARNING JOURNAL

As you work through this Learning Short-take®, make detailed notes on this page of the lessons you have learned and any useful skill areas. For each lesson or refresher point think about how you could further develop this skill. Your coach will want to discuss these with you in your Skill Development Action Planning meeting.

*"…that is what learning is.
You suddenly understand something you've understood all your life, but in a new way."*

DORIS LESSING

"Act as though it were impossible to fail."

WINSTON CHURCHILL

> *"The wise do at once what the fool does later."*
> BALTASAR GRACIAN (1601-58), SPANISH JESUIT PRIEST AND AUTHOR.

Learning or Idea	Action to be taken	Result Expected

The correct strategy for Americans negotiating with Japanese or other foreign clients is a Japanese strategy: ask questions. When you think you understand, ask more questions. Carefully feel for pressure points. If an impasse is reached, don't pressure. Suggest a recess or another meeting.

JOHN L. GRAHAM

Section 3

SKILL DEVELOPMENT ACTION PLAN

Your Skill Development Action Plan is the last Step in the process. After you have completed the Learning Short-take® and all Activities, update your Learning Journal, then complete this section.

SKILL DEVELOPMENT ACTION PLAN

This is the most important part of the program - your individual Skill Development Action Plan.

You need to complete this plan before meeting with your manager or prior to on-going coaching. You will discuss it in detail with your manager or coach as he or she will ensure that you have everything you need to complete the tasks and activities.

Once you have completed your **Skill Development Action Plan** schedule a meeting time with your manager or coach to review your plan. Take your Learning Short-take® and all other documentation received during the training course to this meeting.

Remember - you have committed to your **Skill Development Action Plan**, and need to make time to complete your tasks!

"The mind, once stretched by a new idea, never regains its original dimensions."

OLIVER WENDELL HOLMES

"Whatever you can do or dream you can - begin it. Boldness has genius, power and magic."

JOHANN WOLFGANG VON GOETHE

"Imagination is the eye of the soul."
JOSEPH JOUBERT (1754-1824)

Task or activity (Be specific)	Measure (this will help you to know you have achieved it)	Date (Be specific)
Reflect on your Learning Journal. Transfer action items that you can apply to your job. Ensure that you include some 'stretch goals' and also a blend of short, medium and long term goals.	Apart from you, who else is needed to assist you in achieving your goal.	Be specific. A general date such as 'Quarter 1', 'August', or 'by end of year' is vague and more likely to result in not achieving your target. Be specific – e.g. 22nd November.

IDEAS FOR DISCUSSION WITH MY MANAGER

Ideas

CONGRATULATIONS!

You've now completed this Learning Short-take®.

Meet with your Manager/Coach to discuss your Skill Development Action Plan.

Further Reading

'Getting to Yes' by Roger Fisher, William Ury, Bruce Patton - 1994 - 207 pages

"The first principle of contract negotiation is don't remind them of what you did in the past; tell them what you're going to do in the future."

STAN MUSIAL

QUICK REFERENCE

This Quick Reference provides you with a summary of key concepts, models and reference material from Learning Short-takes®. We have also included some quotations to ponder.

Use this section as a quick reference to keep your learning active.

Quick Reference

Most business people negotiate something on a daily basis.
To negotiate is to seek mutual agreement through an exchange of dialogue.

Sales vs. Negotiation

Selling involves interacting with prospective customers and offering them products or services that fulfill their needs.

Negotiation is the process whereby two or more parties consent to bargaining, in order to arrive at a mutually acceptable solution regarding the rate of exchange of specific items or services.

Quick Reference

What negotiation isn't

The end game in negotiation isn't getting your way, it's constructing a "deal" that satisfies the needs and wants of everyone.

The Win/Win Model

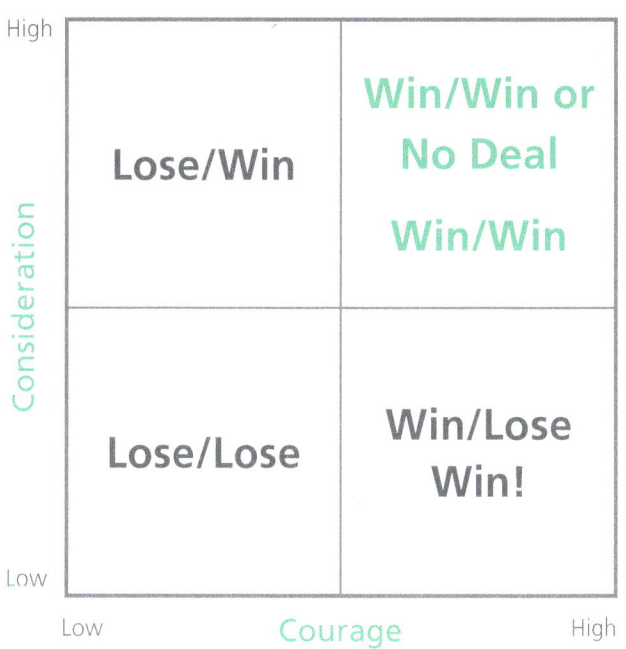

7 Habits of Highly Effective People, Covey, S.

Quick Reference

Win/Win

- Agreements or solutions are mutually beneficial.
- A belief in the Third Alternative - A better way.

Win/Lose

- Use of position, power, credentials, possessions or personality to get one's way.
- The win/lose mentality is dysfunctional to interdependence.

Lose/Win

- Lose/Win people are quick to please or appease.
- Capitulation - giving in or giving up.

Many executives, managers and parents oscillate between Win/Lose and Lose/Win.

Lose/Lose

- Result of encounters between two Win/Lose individuals.
- Also the philosophy of highly dependent people.

Win

- Win at all costs. Other people don't matter.
- The most common approach in everyday negotiation.

Quick Reference

Win/Win or No Deal

- If we can't find a solution that would benefit both parties, we agree to disagree.

- Most realistic at the beginning of a relationship or enterprise.

5 Dimensions of Win/Win

1. Character

2. Relationship

3. Agreements

4. Supportive Systems

5. Processes.

Quick Reference

*There are two fools in every market.
One asks too little, one asks too much.*

RUSSIAN PROVERB

Positional Bargaining vs. Principled Negotiation

Positional bargaining is demanding, adversarial and unyielding.

Principled Negotiation is based on:

1. Mutual Trust
2. A positive relationship
3. Shared interests (goals and objectives)
4. Satisfactory zone of possible agreement

Quick Reference

Preparing for Negotiation

Use the Negotiation Planner to assist you when preparing for a negotiation.

Download it now:

https://www.catherinemattiske.com/books

"

*Let us never negotiate out of fear.
But let us never fear to negotiate.*

JOHN FITZGERALD KENNEDY
(AMERICAN 35TH US PRESIDENT)

"

Quick Reference

The Negotiation Process

1. Interests
2. Options
3. Standards
4. People
5. BATNA
6. Closure

Element 1 - Interests

Understand your interests before continuing a negotiation

- Underlying motivations
- Needs and concerns
- Fears and aspirations

Uncovering Interests

- Look behind positions for underlying interests
- Put your self in the other person's shoes
- Ask "why?"
- Ask "why not?"
- "What could be wrong with…?

Quick Reference

Element 2 - Inventing Options for Mutual Gain

- Focus the group on the objective of the negotiation
- Respect the group
- Take your time, don't push too hard
- Focus on the future

Idea Growers

- What have we missed?
- What would happen if…
- What else would be affected by this change?
- What questions are there?
- Why do we do it this way?
- How could we improve…?
- and Thank You.

Element 3 - Standards

The solution is to negotiate on some basis independent of the will of either side, that is, on the basis of objective criteria.

Quick Reference

Element 4 - People

People Checklist for Success

- Other side - people just like you
- Be empathic and assertive
- Focus on the issue not the person
- Balance emotion with reason
- Tactfully question
- Actively listen
- Observe carefully
- Ensure mutual understanding
- Don't buy the relationship

Element 5 - BATNA

Develop Your BATNA - Best Alternative to a Negotiated Agreement

Your BATNA is your walk away position. This is the standard against which any proposed agreement should be measured.

Quick Reference

How to Negotiate with a Customer You Can't Afford to Lose

- When under attack, LISTEN!
- Keep the customer talking.
- Keep track of issues requiring negotiation.
- Assert your needs!
- Commit to a solution only after it's certain to work for both parties.
- Save the hardest issues for last.
- Start high and concede slowly.

Element 6 - Close

People Checklist for Success

- Think about closure before you begin
- List the issues of both sides
- Draft a framework
- Improve as you go
- Create emotional commitment
- Fill in details before you commit
- Don't commit until the end

"

Never forget the power of silence, that massively disconcerting pause which goes on and on and may at last induce an opponent to babble and backtrack nervously.

LANCE MORROW

"

NEXT STEPS

Congratulations! You have now completed this Learning Short-take® title. The entire list of Learning Short-takes® can be found on the catherinemattiske.com website.

In this section we have suggested Learning Short-take® titles for you that will build your learning. You may order these Learning Short-takes® online at https://www.catherinemattiske.com/books or from your bookstores.

Understanding Customer Motivation
Get Inside the Customer's Mind

Learning Short-take® Outline

Understanding Customer Motivation combines self-study with real workplace activities to help you understand the key elements that motivate customers. You will learn specific techniques to encourage your customers to start or continue to do business with you and to provide them with the products and services that they need. **Understanding Customer Motivation** investigates the importance of creating value for customers, why customers buy, the impact and influences of buying objectives, the four customer types, adapting the selling process, and a process for identifying value opportunities in your business.

Customers are interested in products and services that fulfill their needs and wants. If a customer doesn't have a perceived need or want, then it is unlikely that they will buy. As an experienced salesperson, you will appreciate the importance of need creation in motivating customers to want to own or use the products and services that you sell. By examining the psychology and critical motivators of buying, **Understanding Customer Motivation** will assist you in garnering new and recurring customers and preserving positive customer relationships.

Understanding Customer Motivation includes the **Value Identification Tool** and the **True Motivators Reminder Card**, provided as free downloadable tools.

Learning Objectives

- Explain the psychology of buying and the elements of customer motivation.
- Explain the importance of creating value for customers and the impact on customer motivation.
- Identify value opportunities in your business.
- Explain why customers buy and the impact of buying objectives and buying influences.
- Develop strategies for aligning customer behavior types with need creation opportunities.
- Create a Skill Development Action Plan.

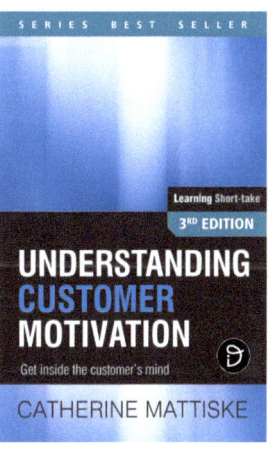

Course Content

- Part 1: Getting Started
- Part 2: Psychology of Buying
- Part 3: Why Customers Buy
- Part 4: Theories of Motivation
- Part 5: 7 Service Principles
- Part 6: Customer Types

Understanding Relationship Selling
How to Build Customer's Rapport, Respect & Trust

Learning Short-take® Outline

Understanding Relationship Selling combines self-study with realistic workplace activities to develop skills in understanding the value of building relationships with your customers to facilitate repeat business and achieve referrals. It compares traditional selling techniques with more modern sales processes based on the development of trust, rapport and empathy. This Learning Short-take® will guide you in evaluating your own approach to selling, and help you develop new and innovative strategies to foster key relationships, understand customer needs, and provide appropriate sales solutions.

Relationship selling is based on the premise that the best source of new business is through existing customers and referrals from existing customers. This approach requires a long-term commitment to providing ongoing customer satisfaction, rather than just a short-term focus on making sales. While relationship selling may take longer to cultivate, the organization will be rewarded with high levels of repeat business, new business and referrals from satisfied customers.

Understanding Relationship Selling includes the **'Relationship Selling' Job Aid**, provided as a free downloadable tool.

Learning Objectives
- Define relationship selling.
- Explain the difference between traditional selling and relationship selling.
- State key differences between product-based selling and needs-based selling.
- Explain the importance of trust in relationship selling.
- Explain the principles of relationship selling.
- Describe how to maintain a relationship even when the answer is 'no'.
- Identify the steps in the relationship selling process.
- Create a Skill Development Action.

Course Content
- Part 1: Traditional versus modern approaches to selling
- Part 2: Evolution of the selling function
- Part 3: Inside the sales call
- Part 4: Principles of relationship selling
- Part 5: Relationship builders and relationship breakers
- Part 6: Top ten tips for relationship selling

Influencing for Opportunity
Identify and Maximize Ways to Influence

Course Content

- Part 1: Fundamentals of Influence
- Part 2: Influence: A Choice
- Part 3: Naturally Occurring Influence Patterns
- Part 4: Methods of Persuasion
- Part 5: The Challenges of Influence
- Part 6: Building a life of Influence

Learning Short-take® Outline

Influencing for Opportunity combines self-study with realistic workplace activities to provide you with the key skills and techniques to influence those around you. You will learn the theory of influence, influence principles and strategies, as well as how to plan and prepare for important opportunities to influence. As a result, you should achieve greater results in your organization, work more productively and effectively in a team environment, and develop stronger working relationships with co-workers, suppliers and customers.

The ability to influence others is critical in today's competitive business environment. Being highly skilled in influence enables you to build the relationships you need to get results inside or outside the organization. Employees and managers alike cannot assume they have power over others - they must earn it through influence. Being an influential person is a skill that can be learned and practiced. **Influencing for Opportunity** will help you succeed in the modern corporate environment by increasing your ability to influence others.

Influencing for Opportunity includes a **toolkit of job aids and learning support tools** provided to you as free downloads.

Learning Objectives

- Identify patterns of influence.
- Evaluate how you currently use influence behaviors and identify areas for development.
- Develop influence behaviors for greater personal and business success.
- Establish clear and powerful influence goals.
- Increase influence to overcome resistance.
- Describe how to ask for and receive support.
- Design an approach for formal and informal influence situations; apply the approach to a real-life situation.
- Create a Skill Development Action Plan.

www.catherinemattiske.com

www.ingramcontent.com/pod-product-compliance
Lightning Source LLC
Chambersburg PA
CBHW040002110526
44587CB00001BA/19